Explore!
ROMANS

Jane Bingham

WAYLAND

First published in 2014 by Wayland

Copyright © Wayland 2014

Wayland
Level 17/207 Kent Street
Sydney, NSW 2000

Produced for Wayland by
White-Thomson Publishing
www.wtpub.co.uk
+44 (0)843 208 7460

Editor: Jane Bingham
Designer: Elaine Wilkinson
Picture researcher: Jane Bingham
Illustrations for step-by-step: Stefan Chabluk
Map illustration: Wayland
Proof reader: Lucy Ross

A cataloguing record for this title is available
from the British Library.

ISBN 978 0 7502 8098 3

Dewey Number 937-dc23

Printed in China.

Wayland is a division of Hachette Children's
Books, an Hachette UK company

www.hachette.co.uk

Picture acknowledgements:
The author and publisher would like to thank the
following agencies and people for allowing these
pictures to be reproduced:
Cover (top left) Pierre-Jean Durieu/Shutterstock;
(top right) Dvmsimages/Dreamstime; (bottom left)
Viacheslav Lopatin/Shutterstock; (bottom right)
Dimedrol68/Shutterstock; p.1(left) Collpicto/
Shutterstock; (right) Durdenimages/Dreamstime;
p.3 PerseoMedusa/Shutterstock; p.4 Skoda/
Shutterstock; p.5 (top) Wikimedia; (bottom) mdgn/
Shutterstock; p.6 Andrei Nekrassov/Shutterstock;
p.7 (top) Wikimedia; (bottom) alessandro0770/
Shutterstock; p.8 Lagui/ Shutterstock; p.9
(top) Federico Rostango/Shutterstock; (middle)
Wikimedia; (bottom) Simonhs/Dreamstime; p.11
(top) meunierd/Shutterstock; (middle) Neftali/
Shutterstock; (bottom) Collpicto/Shutterstock;
p.12 perspectivestock/Shutterstock; p.13 (top)
PerseoMedusa/Shutterstock; (bottom) Khirman
Vladimir/Shutterstock; p.14 Wikimedia; p.15 (top)
Wikimedia; (bottom) Neilneil/Dreamstime; p.16
Wikimedia; p.17 (top) Nancypitman/Dreamstime;
(bottom) Wikimedia; p.18 Louvre, Paris, France/
Giraudon/The Bridgeman Art Library; p.19
(left) Alessandro Colle/Shutterstock; (right)
Wikimedia; p.20 artjazz/Shutterstock; p.21 (top)
Route66/Shutterstock; (bottom) Dreamstime/
Durdenimages; p.22 Filip Fuxa/Shutterstock;
p.23 (top) Pavel Ilyukhin/Shutterstock; (bottom)
Wikimedia; p.24 Ken Durden/Shutterstock;
p.25 (top) mountainpix/Shutterstock; (bottom)
duncan1890/istock; p.26 Laurence Gough/
Shutterstock; p.28 (top) Neilneil/Dreamstime;
(bottom) artjazz/Shutterstock; p.29 (top)
alessandro0770/Shutterstock; (middle)
Eurobanks/Dreamstime; (bottom) Rannoch/
Dreamstime; p.31 (top) Wikimedia; (bottom)
Lagui/ Shutterstock; p.32 Ken Durden/
Shutterstock.

The website addresses (URLs) included in this book were valid at
the time of going to press. However, because of the nature of the
Internet, it is possible that some addresses may have changed, or
sites may have changed or closed down since publication. While
the author and publisher regret any inconvenience this may cause
to the readers, no responsibility for any such changes can be
accepted by either the author or the publisher.

Contents

Who were the Romans?

The Roman civilization began in central Italy around 750BCE. It grew into a mighty empire with the city of Rome at its heart. At its largest size, the Roman Empire was home to 65 million people. It collapsed in 476CE, but its influence has continued right up to the present day.

The Roman way of life

Wherever the Romans went, they took their way of life. They built towns and cities, forts and farms, and constructed roads and bridges. All over the Empire, people had to learn Latin, obey Roman laws and worship Roman gods – whether they liked it or not!

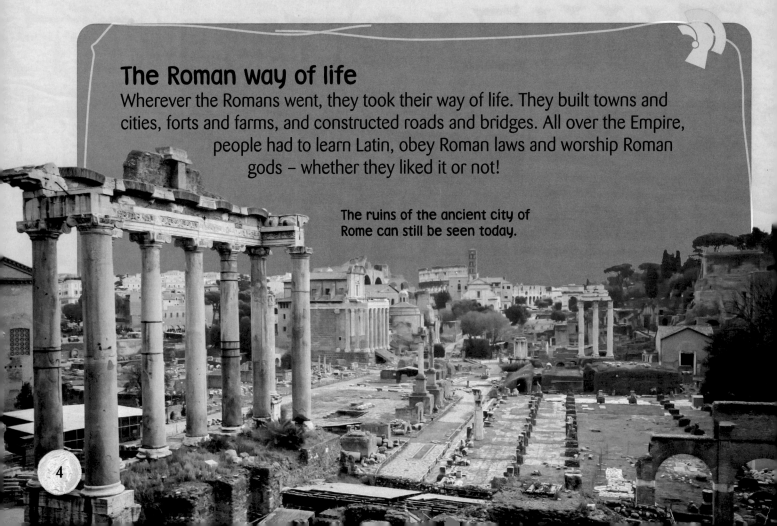

The ruins of the ancient city of Rome can still be seen today.

This portrait of a Roman couple was found in Pompeii. The man holds a scroll and the woman has a stylus and wax tablet for writing.

Lasting evidence

The Romans left plenty of evidence of their way of life. We can study their buildings, art and literature and the work of Roman craftworkers. But perhaps the best evidence of all comes from the town of Pompeii, in southern Italy. In 79CE Mount Vesuvius, a huge volcano, erupted suddenly, burying Pompeii in molten lava. Many centuries later, it was discovered that the town had been preserved almost perfectly, providing a remarkable record of everyday Roman life.

What did the Romans do for us?

Even though the Romans lived two thousand years ago, they still have an impact on the way we live today. In the twenty-first century, architects still design buildings in the Roman style and engineers use Roman techniques and methods. Politicians and lawyers follow practices established in Roman times. Most European languages have their roots in Latin and we use the Roman alphabet whenever we read or write.

The Capitol building in Washington DC is built in a classical, Roman style. It is home to the US government, including the Senate. The American Senate is modelled on the Roman Senate, a group of men who governed Rome for 500 years.

The rise of Rome

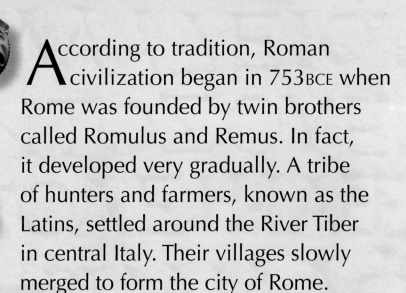

According to tradition, Roman civilization began in 753BCE when Rome was founded by twin brothers called Romulus and Remus. In fact, it developed very gradually. A tribe of hunters and farmers, known as the Latins, settled around the River Tiber in central Italy. Their villages slowly merged to form the city of Rome.

This famous statue shows Romulus and Remus being fed by a wolf. In the Roman legend, the twin founders of Rome were brought up by a wolf until they were rescued by a shepherd.

The Roman Republic

At first, Rome was ruled by kings, but around 500BCE, it became a republic (a state without a king). The Roman Republic was governed by the Senate, a group of 300 men who shared the job of ruling the Roman people. The Republic lasted for almost 500 years. During this time, trading flourished and the army gained control of most of the lands around the Mediterranean Sea.

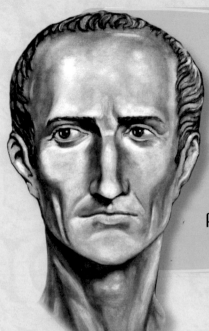

Julius Caesar

As Rome grew richer, the senators quarrelled over how the Republic should be run. The crisis came in 49BCE, when a general called Julius Caesar used his army to seize control of Rome. Caesar restored peace in Rome and passed laws to help the poor. However, some senators feared he had too much power and plotted to kill him.

Julius Caesar was a brilliant army commander who conquered large parts of France and Germany. He wrote many books about his battles.

The Empire is born

After the death of Julius Caesar, there were more struggles for power. In 31BCE, Caesar's adopted son, Octavian, defeated his rival, Mark Anthony, and won control of Rome. Octavian took the name of Augustus, which means 'deeply respected one'. He became the first Roman emperor.

Emperor Augustus was a great soldier as well as an inspiring leader. He is shown here as an army general.

A mighty power

Augustus was the first in a long line of emperors who ruled until the collapse of Rome. They were supposed to govern with the help of the Senate, but in fact they had complete power.

Good and bad emperors

Some emperors ruled wisely. Trajan, Hadrian and Marcus Aurelius treated the Senate with respect. They expanded the Empire, helped the poor, and paid for great public buildings. However, other emperors were cruel and selfish. Tiberius, Nero and Commodus spent a fortune on palaces and feasts, and anyone they disliked was instantly put to death. Emperor Caligula was believed by many to be insane. He once made his soldiers attack the ocean because he was angry with Neptune, god of the sea.

Emperor Nero (54–68CE) sent hundreds of Christians to their death, and even had his wife and mother murdered.

Emperor Trajan (98-117ce) is shown on this coin. He paid for many grand buildings in Rome, and the ruins of Trajan's Market can still be seen today (above).

The Empire weakens

By the third century CE, the Empire was under attack from warlike tribes (nicknamed 'barbarians' by the Romans). The emperors struggled to keep control and in 284CE Diocletian decided to split the Empire in two, with separate rulers for east and west. The Empire stayed divided until 321CE, when Constantine reunited the two halves. He moved his capital from Rome to Byzantium, on the Black Sea, and rebuilt the city, naming it Constantinople after himself.

The end of the Empire

In 395CE, the Roman Empire split permanently into east and west. While the eastern Empire remained strong, waves of barbarians invaded the western Empire. By 410CE, tribes were attacking Rome and in 476CE a barbarian chief declared himself King of Italy. This marked the end of the western Roman Empire, although the eastern Empire lasted for another thousand years, becoming known as the Byzantine Empire.

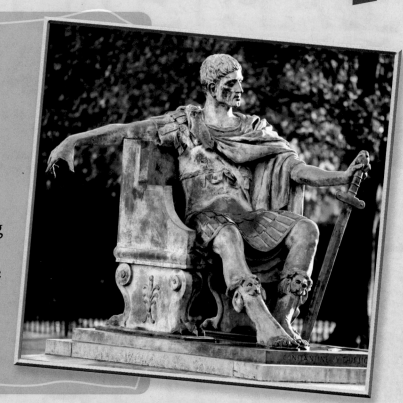

Emperor Constantine (306–337ce) ruled from Constantinople and built up the strength of the eastern Empire.

The Roman world

The Roman Empire reached its largest size in 117CE. At that time, it stretched for 4,000 kilometres (2,500 miles) from east to west, and from Britain in the north to Egypt in the south.

Roman lands

BRITAIN

GERMANY

ASIA

EUROPE

FRANCE

SPAIN

ITALY

Mediterranean Sea

ARABIA

AFRICA

EGYPT

This map shows the Roman Empire at its largest.

Running the Empire

The Empire was divided into provinces, such as Britain and Gaul (France). Each province was ruled by a governor who reported to Rome and controlled the army. Underneath him were the local governors who ran the law courts and collected taxes. Britain had 14 local governors.

The Roman Army fought and worked in highly disciplined groups. These modern actors are dressed as Roman soldiers.

The Roman Army

The key to the Empire's success was its army. Once they had conquered new lands, soldiers constructed forts, roads and bridges and helped to build new towns. They defended the Empire's borders from enemy attacks and put down any rebellions against Roman rule. The Roman Army also captured prisoners of war, who were sold as slaves. Slaves often ended up in distant parts of the Empire, thousands of miles from where they had been born.

Trade and travel

The Empire offered great opportunities for trade. Merchants from different provinces exchanged their goods and vast quantities of food were sent to Rome. Grain, olive oil and wine were in constant demand, and there was a busy trade in wool from Britain, spices from Asia, and gold from Africa. Traders travelled by road, river or sea, and some adventurous merchants reached as far as Scandinavia and Russia.

In 122CE Emperor Hadrian gave orders for a wall to be built across northern England. Hadrian's Wall marked the northern limit of the Romans' lands.

Town and country

Wealthy Romans divided their time between a comfortable town house and a large country villa. Poor people were not so fortunate. Most of them lived in crowded apartments in town or in tiny huts in the country.

Town life

Town houses for the wealthy were built around a central garden. They had private rooms for the family and several large rooms for entertaining guests. In contrast, poor families were often crammed into a single room in an apartment block (called an *insula*). There were no toilets or cooking stoves and people had to buy their food from stalls on the street.

The remains of a street in Pompeii. People used stepping stones to cross the street.

Shops and workshops

Roman city streets were lined with shops and workshops. Bakers, brewers and butchers all had permanent shops, while fruit and vegetables were sold in markets. Craftworkers produced a range of goods from everyday pots to fine ornaments. Workshops were often run as a family business, with adults and children working together.

Pottery jars like these would have been on sale in city workshops.

This mosaic comes from a Roman villa in North Africa. It shows the villa surrounded by its gardens.

Country life

Roman villas were working farmhouses, but they were also luxurious homes, decorated with frescoes and mosaics. In the summer months, villa owners enjoyed their shady gardens, fountains and pools. In the winter, they were kept warm by roaring fires and under-floor heating. Many villas had their own set of baths where the family and guests could relax.

Hundreds of people were needed to run a large villa farm. Some farm workers were local men and women, who were paid a very small wage. Others were slaves who belonged to the villa's owner. Most slaves had no family home. They slept in dormitories, filled with rows of beds.

Family and school

Family life was very important to the Romans. Children, parents and grandparents all shared the family home, and cousins, uncles and aunts sometimes lived there too. At the head of the family was the father, or *paterfamilias*. It was his duty to look after everyone in the home, including the household slaves.

Women

Roman wives had to make sure their household ran smoothly. For rich women this meant supervising their slaves, but poorer women did all the housework themselves. Most Roman women stayed at home or helped in the family business, but there are records of female acrobats, musicians and priestesses.

A gravestone showing a soldier and his family. The children hold a toy sword and a doll.

These wealthy children are riding
a toy chariot pulled by tame birds.

Children's toys

Young children had fun
playing with toys. Wealthy
boys and girls had see-saws
and swings, and even miniature
chariots. Poorer children
played with simple toys, such
as balls, dolls, spinning tops
and wooden swords.

Education

Children from poor families started
work as soon as possible, but richer
parents often sent their children
to school. Girls and boys went to
a primary school, or *ludus*, where
they learned reading, writing and
arithmetic. A slave called a *pedagogus*
took them to school and made sure
they did their schoolwork.

After primary school, girls stayed at
home and prepared for marriage.
Some boys went on to a secondary
school, or *grammaticus*. There they
studied literature, maths, history
and music, trained in athletics and
practised public speaking.

This fragment of a Roman mosaic shows
a slave at work. Slaves worked very
hard to keep rich families in comfort.

Religion and worship

For most of the Roman period, people worshipped many gods. Jupiter was the chief god, while Juno, his wife, was the goddess of women. People prayed to Mars for victory in war, to Minerva for wisdom, and to Venus for success in love. Even the Roman emperors were worshipped as gods.

Temples and sacrifices

The Romans built grand temples for their gods. Only priests were allowed inside, but large crowds gathered around the temple steps to watch priests sacrifice animals to the gods. People believed that these sacrifices would encourage the gods to give them help and protection.

A copy of a Roman statue of Jupiter. He holds the figure of Victory in his hand.

Household gods

Each family home had a small shrine dedicated to their household gods. These friendly spirits, known as the *lares*, were believed to guard and protect the home. The family gathered at their shrine for daily prayers and offered gifts of wine and food to the *lares*.

A shrine to the household gods, found in a house in Pompeii.

Saint Paul was one of the first to spread the Christian message. He travelled to many places in the Roman Empire before he was arrested in Rome and put to death around 67CE.

The coming of Christianity

During the first century CE, the new religion of Christianity began to spread across the Empire. Some emperors saw Christians as dangerous rebels and had them put to death. But in spite of this persecution, Christianity flourished and in 391CE it became the official religion of the Empire.

A Roman child's day

This fictional diary entry describes a day in the life of a wealthy Roman girl.

I wake up when Paulina comes to help me dress. I've known her all my life so she is more like a friend than a slave. I put on my stola and palla (dress and shawl) and Paulina helps me tie up my hair. Until I am married I have to wear white but then I can dress in brighter colours.

Once I am dressed I join the rest of our family for prayers at our household shrine. I show great respect to my parents and grandparents, as I have been taught to do.

After prayers I eat a little bread and honey. Then I walk to school with my brothers and our pedagogus. He stays with us in school and beats us when we don't work hard enough! At school we practise reading and writing. I make a mistake on my wax tablet and have to scrape off all my writing and start again!

By the time I get home, I am tired and hungry, but I feel much better when I see what has been prepared for dinner. We are eating roast pigeon, eggs and lentils – my favourite!

The diary entry on these pages has been written for this book. Can you create your own diary entry for a boy or girl slave in Roman times? Use the facts in this book and in other sources to help you write about a day in their life.

Entertainment and leisure

Most Romans had plenty of leisure time, especially in the later years of the Empire. Working hours were short, slaves did much of the work, and there were many public holidays. People flocked to public shows, generally known as 'the games'. They enjoyed chariot races and plays, and liked to relax in the public baths.

The Colosseum was home to the games in Rome. Sometimes the arena was flooded with water for a sea battle!

The games

Roman emperors paid for spectacular shows to be held in vast stone stadiums, known as amphitheatres. The games included acrobatic displays, music and dancing, but the most popular acts were the violent ones, such as animal hunts, gladiator fights and mock battles. As part of the day's entertainment, criminals and Christians were executed – many were mauled to death by lions.

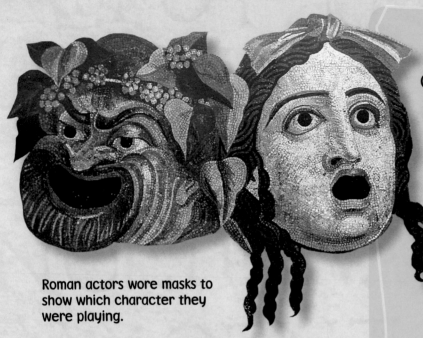

Roman actors wore masks to show which character they were playing.

Races and plays

Chariot-racing was a very popular sport. The races were wild and dangerous and chariot drivers were often killed. Plays were usually performed in outdoor stone theatres, and people could choose to watch a comedy, a tragedy or a mime. Mimes were simple plays in which a chorus sang a series of songs while actors mimed the actions.

The baths

All Roman towns and cities had a set of public baths, where people went to get clean and to meet their friends. Bathers moved through a series of hot and cool pools, and they could also enjoy a massage, spend time in the steam room and work out in the exercise yard. When they had finished bathing, people could buy a snack at a food stall, read in the library or simply relax in the gardens.

The remains of a set of Roman baths have survived in the city of Bath in southern England.

Building technology

Roman architects and engineers made enormous advances in building technology, inventing new techniques and materials that are still used today.

The aqueduct at Pont du Gard was part of a system for carrying water from the mountains to the city of Nîmes, in southern France.

Useful arches

The Romans developed a new way of building, using arches and columns. Arches are extremely strong because each stone pushes against the stones on either side of it. This sideways pressure holds arches together firmly, making them strong enough to support another set of columns and arches above them. By using these new structures, the Romans could build enormous public buildings, as well as bridges and viaducts that spanned wide valleys.

The Pantheon in Rome was built from brick filled with concrete. Once the building was finished, the walls were lined with stone.

Using concrete

Roman builders invented concrete! They mixed volcanic ash with water and added small stones to make a building material that was strong but very light. Walls were built with a double shell of bricks and the space between the bricks was filled up with concrete (rather like the filling in a sandwich). It set rock-hard, making the walls immensely strong without adding lots of extra weight.

Amazing engineers

Roman engineers built roads that ran straight though a landscape. They designed bridges to cross wide valleys, and aqueducts to carry water for hundreds of kilometres. Water systems in towns supplied the public baths and fountains while a network of underground channels carried away sewage and waste. The Romans also invented a method of under-floor heating, called the hypocaust. A furnace in the basement sent warm air through spaces underneath the floor.

The floor of a Roman building, showing the spaces where air could circulate. Warm air from a furnace flowed through the spaces to warm up the floor.

Artists and writers

The Romans were surrounded by art. Temples, palaces and villas had frescoes on their walls and mosaics on their floors. Towns and cities were filled with statues of emperors, gods and heroes.

Sculptors
Sculptors created figures in bronze, stone and marble, and carved lively scenes on buildings. Statues of emperors usually showed perfect beings, but some sculpted portraits gave a more realistic picture of how people really looked.

A sculpted bronze figure of the Emperor Marcus Aurelius. He wrote books on philosophy as well as ruling the Empire.

Painters

Artists painted colourful frescoes on villa walls. Their subjects included bold architectural designs, stories of the gods, and scenes from daily life. Many Romans paid for their portraits to be painted on wooden panels and the walls of some family homes were lined with paintings of their ancestors.

The walls of country villas were often painted with garden scenes.

Writers

The Roman period was an outstanding time for literature. Historians such as Livy, Plutarch and Suetonius described the great events and figures of their age. Virgil's long poem, the *Aeneid*, told the amazing adventures of Aeneas of Troy, and Ovid's *Metamorphoses* brought the Roman myths to life. Horace wrote moving love poems, Cicero composed rousing speeches, and Pliny's lively letters include an exciting account of the eruption of Mount Vesuvius. Great works like these are still studied, admired and enjoyed today.

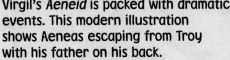

Virgil's *Aeneid* is packed with dramatic events. This modern illustration shows Aeneas escaping from Troy with his father on his back.

Make a mosaic

Roman mosaics were made from thousands of tiny tiles, called *tesserae*. Their subjects ranged from simple geometric patterns to elaborate scenes. You can make your own mosaic with a simple face design.

You will need:

paper plate

three sheets of coloured paper

glue

scissors

ruler

pencil

This Roman mosaic shows the head of Medusa, a terrifying monster with snakes instead of hair.

1 Use your ruler to draw a grid of 10 mm squares on your sheets of coloured paper. Then cut out your squares.

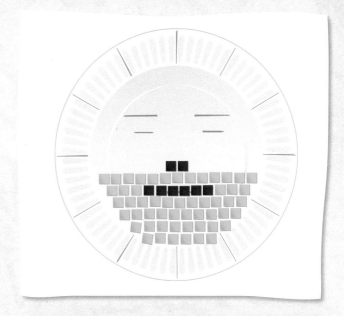

2 Draw a simple face on your plate, using only straight lines. This is a rough guide for you to follow.

3 Stick your paper tiles over your design. Start at the bottom of the face and work up. Do the outer rim last.

4 Keep going until you have covered the plate. You need to be careful and take your time. Imagine how long it took the Romans to cover a whole floor!

27

Facts and figures

In the mid 2nd century CE, around 65 million people lived inside the borders of the Roman Empire – more than a third of the world's total population.

It has been estimated that over a quarter of the population of Ancient Rome were slaves.

The Colosseum in Rome was the largest building in the Roman Empire. It had 76 entrance gates and room for 50,000 spectators. To mark its opening in 80CE, there were 100 days of non-stop games. Around 9,000 wild animals died in the opening games.

The Romans didn't have soap. Instead they covered their bodies with oil, then they scraped it off with a curved metal tool called a *strigil*. When they removed the oil, the dirt came off with it!

The calendar we use today is based on the Roman calendar, and some of our months are named after Roman gods or rulers. March and June get their names from Mars and Juno. July and August were named after Julius Caesar and the Emperor Augustus.

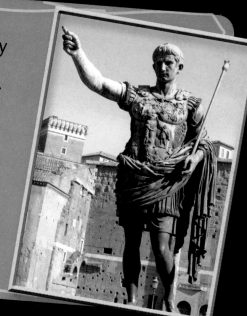

The Romans were famous for their amazing feasts. Hosts competed with each other to serve up unusual dishes such as elephants' trunks, ostriches' brains and flamingos' tongues!

Some women fought as gladiators in the games. But many Romans objected to women fighting and in 20CE female gladiators were banned.

Roman soldiers sometimes advanced in a formation called the *testudo*, or tortoise. They locked their shields together to form a solid barrier over their heads and around the edges of the group.

Glossary

apartment A room or set of rooms where people live, inside a building that contains many homes. Another word for apartment is flat.

architectural To do with the design and construction of buildings.

barbarian A member of a tribe that does not belong to an ancient civilization.

BCE The letters BCE stand for 'before common era'. They refer to dates before the birth of Christ.

CE The letters CE stand for 'common era'. They refer to dates after the birth of Christ.

civilization A well-organized society.

dormitory A large room with lots of beds where many people sleep.

evidence Objects, buildings or other information that show the truth about something.

fictional Made up or invented.

fort A very strong building used as a base by soldiers to defend a place.

founded Started or set up.

fresco Designs, scenes or figures that are painted directly onto walls.

gladiator Someone who is trained to fight against others as a form of entertainment.

influence To have an effect on someone or something.

lava Liquid rock that comes from the inside of a volcano.

mime To act a part in a play by using actions and movements but no words.

molten Liquid or melted.

pedagogus A family slave who took the children to and from school and looked after them there. Sometimes, a *pedagogus* also acted as a teacher at home.

persecution Very cruel treatment of people, often because of their beliefs.

philosophy The study of the meaning of life.

republic A state with a ruler who is voted for by the people.

Senate A group of people who are voted for by the people and who play an important role in ruling a country.

shrine A place or a building where people offer gifts and prayers to gods.

stylus A pointed metal stick used by the Romans to write on wax tablets.

Further reading

Ancient Rome (Men, Women and Children),
Jane Bingham (Wayland, 2009)

In Roman Britain (Men, Women and Children),
Jane Bingham (Wayland, 2011)

The Romans (History from Objects),
John Malam (Wayland, 2012)

The Romans (The Gruesome Truth About),
Jillian Powell (Wayland, 2010)

Ancient Romans (Craft Box), Jillian Powell
(Wayland, 2013)

Websites

http://www.bbc.co.uk/schools/primaryhistory/romans/
A BBC website for children, with features on many aspects of
Roman life including the army, technology, leisure, and family life.
You can also play an interactive game on Roman archaeology.

http://www.roman-empire.net/children/
A site on the Romans with many sections. It includes a children's
section with a feature on the cartoon character of Asterix.

http://www.pbs.org/empires/romans/index.html
An American PBS website that traces the history of the Romans,
including sections on the emperors, religion, and daily life.

http://www.bbc.co.uk/history/ancient/romans/questions_01.shtml
A detailed site on Roman Britain. It includes a feature for children on a
day in the life of a 10-year-old in Roman Britain.

Index

Explore!

Who were the Victorians?
Queen Victoria's reign
Empire and exploration
Rich and poor
Working life
Health and medicine
A Victorian schoolchild's diary
Scientists and inventors
Engineers and builders
All kinds of transport
Artists, writers and photographers
Make a thaumatrope
Facts and figures

978 0 7502 8037 2

Who were the Romans?
The rise of Rome
A mighty power
The Roman world
Town and country
Family and school
Religion and worship
A Roman child's day
Entertainment and leisure
Building technology
Artists and writers
Make a mosaic
Facts and figures

978 0 7502 8098 3

What was World War One?
The war begins
A terrible struggle
A worldwide war
A soldier's day
New technology
Send a message in Morse code
Planes, airships and submarines
Women at war
On the home front
Picturing the war
After the war
Facts and figures

978 0 7502 8027 3

Who were the Ancient Egyptians?
Early kingdoms
A mighty power
The Egyptian world
Religion and beliefs
Everyday life
A day at a temple school
Feasting and fun
Brilliant buildings
Medicine, science and magic
Art, music and writing
Write in hieroglyphics
Facts and figures

978 0 7502 8097 6

What was World War Two?
The war begins
A worldwide war
The final stages
The holocaust
On the home front
Keeping safe
A letter from wartime London
Science in war
Send a coded message
Technology in war
Picturing the war
Facts and figures

978 0 7502 8038 9

Who were the Ancient Greeks?
Early Greeks
A great civilization
The Greek world
Family life
Gods and goddesses
Games and plays
A day at the Olympic Games
Make a theatrical mask
Maths, science and medicine
Architects and builders
Art and ideas
Facts and figures

978 0 7502 8099 0

Who were the Tudors?
Two powerful kings
Edward, Mary, Elizabeth
Rich and poor
A kitchen-maid's day
Making Tudor gingerbread
Tudor towns
Tudor entertainments
Exploring the world
Traders and settlers
Science and technology
Artists, musicians and writers
Facts and figures

978 0 7502 8036 5

Who was William Shakespeare?
Young William
A great success
All sorts of plays
Shakespeare's England
The wider world
Shakespeare's London
The Globe Theatre
Make a model theatre
Actors and playwrights
A boy actor's day
Music and art
Facts and figures

978 0 7502 8135 5

WAYLAND